Rough Guides

25 Ultimate experiences

Wildlife
Adventures

Make the most of your time on Earth

ROUGH
GUIDES

25 YEARS 1982–2007

NEW YORK • LONDON • DELHI

Contents

Introduction

EXPERIENCES have always been at the heart of the Rough Guide concept. A group of us began writing the books **25 years ago** (hence this celebratory mini series) and wanted to share the kind of travels we had been doing ourselves. It seems bizarre to recall that in the early 1980s, travel was very much a minority pursuit. Sure, there was a lot of tourism around, and that was reflected in the guidebooks in print, which traipsed around the established sights with scarcely a backward look at the local population and their life. We wanted to change all that: to put a country or a city's popular culture centre stage, to highlight the clubs where you could hear local music, drink with people you hadn't come on holiday with, watch the local football, join in with the festivals. And of course we wanted to push travel a bit further, inspire readers with the confidence and knowledge to break away from established routes, to find pleasure and excitement in remote islands, or desert routes, or mountain treks, or in street culture.

Twenty-five years on, that thinking seems pretty obvious: we all want to experience something real about a destination, and to seek out travel's **ultimate experiences**. Which is exactly where these **25 books** come in. They are not in any sense a new series of guidebooks. We're happy with the series that we already have in print. Instead, the **25s** are a collection of ideas, enthusiasms and inspirations: a selection of the very best things to see or do – and not just before you die, but now. Each selection is gold dust. That's the brief to our writers: there is no room here for the average, no space fillers. Pick any one of our selections and you will enrich your travelling life.

But first of all, take the time to browse. Grab a half dozen of these books and let the ideas percolate … and then begin making your plans.

Mark Ellingham
Founder & Series Editor, Rough Guides

Ultimate experiences
Wildlife Adventures

1 Whale-watching in Baja California

Whale shapes are picked out in fairy lights; whalebones are hung on restaurant walls and garden fences; posters, flyers and sandwich boards depict whales outside every shop and bar – even the name of the supermarket here, La Ballena, means whale.

If you didn't already know, you might guess that Guerrero Negro, a flyblown pitstop halfway down the long, spindly peninsula of Baja California, is the main base for whale-watching in Mexico. Every November, California Gray whales leave Alaska en masse and migrate south to calve, arriving in the warm waters of Mexico in January and February.

The lagoon close to Guerrero Negro is where most fetch up – and the tour to see them, with a guaranteed sighting at close quarters, is one of Mexico's most unforgettable experiences.

And it goes like this. By the time the small boat reaches the middle of the glassy-smooth lagoon and the captain switches off the engine, all its excitable passengers have been silenced. Someone spots a distant, cloudy spray – then a great grey body, studded white with barnacles, rises out of the water and curves back in with a deep, resounding splash, leaving a trail of smooth rings across the surface of the water. The little boat rocks and shakes, and curious whales come closer.

Round and round they swim, nine metres of pure elegance twisting, flipping, rolling and spouting, their brand-new offspring gliding alongside – the boat's passengers can almost touch them. And the whales are often joined by dolphins, aquatic bodyguards swimming in perfectly synchronized pairs to protect the whale calves; and by sea-lions, their cheeky whiskered faces nearly stealing the show. Then just as suddenly as the mammals arrived, they disappear back into the deep. The lagoon settles and, moved to silence or even tears, a boatload of awestruck tourists motors back to shore.

Someone spots a distant, cloudy spray – then a great grey body, studded white with barnacles, rises out of the water . . .

need to know Guerrero Negro is easily reached by bus from Tijuana on the US border (7 daily; 10hr) or La Paz at the southern tip of Baja (3 daily; 12hr). There are numerous operators offering whale-watching tours (from $40) in Guerrero Negro and the town of San Ignacio, 150km to the south.

2

Angling for
brown bears
in Alaska

If you've ever seen a photo of a huge brown bear standing knee-deep in rushing water, poised to catch a leaping salmon in its mouth, there's a ninety-five percent chance it was taken at Brooks Falls, a stalling point for the millions of sockeye salmon that make their annual spawning run up the Brooks River. Each July, at the height of the migration, bears flock in to exploit the excellent feeding possibilities, and with viewing platforms set up a few metres from the action, watching them is both exhilarating and slightly nerve-racking – and it's easy to feel as though you're right in the middle of a wildlife documentary. At any one time, you might see a dozen or more jockeying for position. Such proximity causes considerable friction among these naturally solitary animals, but size, age and experience define a hierarchy that allows posturing and roaring to take the place of genuine battles.

Fluffy and defenceless babies are highly vulnerable to fatal attacks from adult males, so the mothers go to great lengths to ensure they're secure, sending their cubs to the topmost branches of nearby trees, and then fishing warily close by. Daring juveniles like to grab the prime fishing spot atop the falls, but become very nervous if bears higher up the pecking order come close – successfully holding pole position might mean moving up the rankings, but the youngster risks a severe beating. Some older and wiser bears prefer wallowing in the pool below the falls: one regular visitor dives down every few minutes and always seems to come up with flapping sockeye in his mouth. Come the end of the salmon run, the bears head for the hills, only to return in September for a final pre-hibernation gorge on the carcasses of the spent fish as they drift downstream.

need to know

Viewing at Brooks Falls (Ⓦ www.nps.gov/katm) is free. The falls are a twenty-minute walk from Brooks Camp, where there's a campsite ($8 per person), upscale cabin accommodation ($250 for two people), and a buffet-style restaurant and bar. Getting to Brooks Camp from Anchorage ($540 round-trip) involves a commercial flight to the town of King Salmon, then a short float-plane flight.

3 Lonesome George
and the
giants of the Galápagos

Of all the Galápagos Islands' assorted animal oddballs, the giant tortoise is king. Symbol and namesake of the archipelago (*galápago* is Spanish for tortoise), this timeworn creature exudes all the authority of a head of state, not to mention a vaguely comical air that's very much part of its charm, with its wizened head, telescopic neck and toothless smile, hoary legs that look better suited to breaststroke than marching over volcanoes, and deliberate, slow-motion movements like a clockwork toy winding down.

Giant tortoises weren't always flavour of the day – or rather they were, literally speaking. Victims, ironically, of their own extraordinary gift for survival, they were taken in their thousands by sailors, upturned and left unfed and unwatered in ships' holds, to be slaughtered months later for fresh meat; on shore, meanwhile, tortoise hatchlings were snaffled up by introduced predators like rats and pigs. Recent conservation efforts have averted a total calamity, but at least three out of the fourteen endemic varieties are now extinct – and that's not counting the inevitable demise of poor old Lonesome George, last survivor of the race from Pinta Island, who's living out the rest of his plentiful days in comfortable captivity, apparently devoid of any desire to start a family with hand-picked brides from other islands.

It stirs the soul to stare into the eyes of an animal that was born long before your grandparents, and which will probably outlive you, too. And as you're in the very place which served as inspiration for the theory of natural selection, it's stranger still to fancy that it might even have brushed carapace with Darwin himself, and unwittingly helped him to unravel what he called the "mystery of mysteries – the first appearance of new beings on this earth".

need to know

Best reached via a flight from Quito
or Guayaquil in Ecuador, the islands
comprise the Galápagos National Park
(www.galapagospark.org), and you'll
have to pay $100 entrance fee on
arrival. Giant tortoises inhabit Isabela,
Santa Cruz, Santiago, San Cristóbal,
Española and Pinzón islands; you can
also see them (and Lonesome George)
at the Charles Darwin Research
Station (Ⓦ www.darwinfoundation.org)
in Puerto Ayora on Santa Cruz.

4 Trekking through the Pantanal wetlands, Brazil

Weary travellers twist in their hammocks as the sun rises; few have slept. All night long, the small campsite glade has resounded with the noise of **snuffling**, **snorting** and **bashing** through the undergrowth, broken only by a hideous high-pitched **yelling** and the sound of **thrashing** water. And then, the deafening **squawking** of the dawn chorus.

"The snuffling?" says one of the gaucho-cum-guides over *cafezinho* coffees and toast. "That's the peccaries. It's normal". And the thrashing water? "Ah, you were lucky. That was an anaconda killing a cow in the stream over there". The stream we waded through last night on a so-called torchlit adventure. "Yes". And the birds? "Parrots – possibly. Parakeets. Or toucans. Storks. Roseate spoonbills. Kingfishers. Snowy egrets. Red crested cardinals . . ."

Some 650 species of bird inhabit the Pantanal, the world's largest freshwater wetland, alongside 3500 plant species, 250 types of fish, 110 kinds of mammal and 50 different reptiles. And when the waters of the Paraguay River recede in April, its grassy plains resemble nothing other than a vast cageless zoo. Caimans, capybaras and giant otters wallow in the murky lagoons and rivers, jaguars and ocelots prowl the long grass, armadillos and anteaters forage for insects. And eight million cows graze.

The gauchos who roam the Pantanal on horseback comprise most of its human population, and they make the most knowledgeable guides. They'll track down flocks of magnificent hyacinth macaws, roosting in trees and preening their violet feathers. They'll wrestle a crocodile out of the water for close-up viewing, or point out the Jabiru stork, as tall as a man, picking its way delicately around the edge of a lily-choked pond. And in the evening they'll invite their visitors to sit round a blazing fire while they play accordions, pass round yerba mate tea and tell derring-do stories of life in the plains of the Pantanal.

need to know

The Pantanal's tourist season is its dry one (April–Oct), when a dozen lodges offer accommodation, meals and tours with gaucho guides; try **Corumbá Tur** (☎ 55/67-231 1532). It's inadvisable to go into the wetlands without a knowledgeable guide or tour company; try **Green Track** (🌐 www.greentrack.net).

5 Following
The *Greatest* Show on Earth,
Tanzania

need to know

As a guide, the best time to see the migration in the Serengeti is between December and July, but the exact movement of the herds varies annually; for the incredible river crossings, visit in June (Grumeti) and July or August (Mara). Check out ⓦwww.wildwatch.com/sightings/migration.asp for up-to-date reports of their current locations.

Imagine squinting into the shimmering Serengeti horizon and seeing a herd of wildebeest trundle into view. They're moving slowly, stopping every now and then to graze on what's left of the parched savannah. At first, they number a couple of dozen, but as you watch, tens become hundreds, and hundreds become thousands. And still they come – a snorting, braying mass, relentlessly marching north in search of food. This is the wildebeest migration, and watching it play out on the sweeping plains of Tanzania's Serengeti National Park is unforgettable.

The statistics are staggering: in May each year, over 2.5 million animals, mostly wildebeest but also several hundred thousand zebra and antelope, set out on a three-month journey from the short-grass plains of the southern Serengeti to Kenya's Maasai Mara Game Reserve. On the way, they'll cover some 800km of open plains and croc-infested rivers, running the gauntlet of predators such as lions, cheetahs, hyenas and hunting dogs.

By June, the herds have passed deep into the park's Western Corridor and are nervously starting to cross the Grumeti River. This is the migration at its most savage – and the defining moment of countless wildlife documentaries – as the reluctant wildebeest gather at the riverbank, too scared to go any further, until the mass behind them is so intense that they spill down into the water and are suddenly swimming, scraping and fighting in a desperate attempt to get across. Many are injured or drowned in the mayhem, while huge Nile crocodiles pick off the weak and unwary.

Those that do make it are still some 65km from the Mara River, the last and brutal barrier between them and the rain-ripened grasses of the Masaai Mara. Once there, they'll have three months to eat their fill before going through it all over again on the return journey south.

Getting cute:
panda cubs in Chengdu, China

6

There's only one thing cuter than a giant panda: its cuddly, bumbling baby, the closest animal equivalent to a real live teddy. But these loveable black-and-white bears are one of the most reproductively challenged species on the planet, with exceptionally low birth rates; it's thought that there are fewer than two thousand of them left worldwide. The Giant Panda Breeding Research Base, just outside Chengdu in Sichuan, was established to preserve this cherished emblem of China, and has become a magnet for panda fans worldwide. It's extremely rare to see a cub in zoos, and it's virtually impossible to see any pandas at all in the wild – but come to the research base and you'll see plenty. And as over eighty cubs have been successfully bred here since 1987, you're almost guaranteed to see youngsters as well as adult bears. Most of the centre is covered in forest to replicate the mountain habitat of the bears, with naturalistic, spacious enclosures replete with trees and pools, and sleeping quarters designed to resemble caves.

There are no bars or railings here; instead, each enclosure is separated from the public pathways by a deep trench – come at feeding time and you can gaze unobstructed as mummy panda languidly chews her way through several heaps of bamboo, slumped nonchalantly on the floor and occasionally throwing a bemused glance at her adoring admirers.

But there's no doubt who steals the show. Panda cubs come charging out of the compounds with surprising energy, romping over the grass and scrambling up the trees, invariably tumbling to the ground again and again as they make hilariously slapstick attempts to reach the top. While the adults like to lounge, babies love to play – and it simply doesn't get any cuter than this.

Need to know

The Chengdu Giant Panda Breeding Research Base (daily 7.30am–6pm; ¥30) is located 10km outside Chengdu in Sichuan province. Feeding time is usually at 10am, and it's also best to visit in winter, as the pandas tend to stay indoors when it gets too hot.

7 **TREKKING** in *Corcovado* National Park, *COSTA RICA*

The road to Corcovado National Park was once paved with gold – lots of gold – and although most of it was carried off by the Diquí Indians, miners still pan here illegally. These days, though, it's just an unpaved track which fords half a dozen rivers during the bone-rattling two-hour ride from the nearest town, Puerto Jiménez, and which runs out at Carate, the southern gateway to the park and a one-horse "town" that comprises just a single store.

The journey in doesn't make an auspicious start to a hike in Corcovado – and it gets worse. Trekking here is not for the faint-hearted: the humidity is 100 percent, there are fast-flowing rivers to cross, and the beach-walking that makes up many of the hikes can only be done at low tide. Cantankerous peccaries roam the woods, and deadly fer-de-lance and bushmaster snakes slip through the shrub.

But you're here because Corcovado is among the most biologically abundant places on earth, encompassing thirteen ecosystems, including lowland rainforests, highland cloud forests, mangrove swamps, lagoons, and coastal and marine habitats. And it's all spectacularly beautiful, even by the high standards of Costa Rica.

Streams trickle down over beaches pounded by Pacific waves, where turtles (hawksbill, leatherback and olive ridley) lay their eggs in the sand and where the shore is dotted with footprints – not human, but tapir, or possibly jaguar. Palm trees hang in bent clumps, and behind them the forest rises up in a sixty metre wall of dense vegetation.

Corcovado has the largest scarlet macaw population in Central America, and the trees flash with bursts of their showy red, blue and yellow plumage. One hotel in the area offers free accommodation if visitors don't see one during their stay – it's never happened. And after the first sighting of the birds flying out from the trees in perfectly co-ordinated pairs, the long journey to reach Corcovado seems a short way to come.

need to know

It's best to visit Corcovado during its dry season (Dec–March). Places in the park's *puestos* (ranger stations with accommodation, showers and meals available) need to be booked six weeks in advance through the Fundación de Parques Nacionales in San Josè (☎ 506/257-2239, ✉ azucena@ns.minae).

8 DIVING IN THE *Red Sea* CORAL GARDENS, EGYPT

Mask on and regulator in place, I'm clinging onto a rail at the stern of the boat, waiting for the signal to step out over the swelling water. It's my first drift dive in what could be a very fast current, fairly daunting for a newly qualified diver who hasn't quite mastered neutral buoyancy. But this is one of the top ten dives in the world, and I'm going to do it, however anxious I feel.

The waves rocking the boat belong to Ras Mohammed National Park, one of the Red Sea's prime diving areas. Of a variety of starting points, the dive instructor chooses Anenome City, a sloping underwater plateau covered with sea anemones hosting cute but ferocious pairs of clownfish. Once we've descended to 20m, we swim across the blue toward Shark Reef. There's no frame of reference now except my buddy: up, down, left and right become meaningless – but for a cloud of silvery jacks and tangle of barracuda circling overhead, there'd be nothing to see at all.

Reaching the 700m vertical wall of Shark Reef, we're suddenly on a virtual conveyor belt, drifting past a kaleidoscopic natural aquarium. Home to countless species, from gaudily striped butterflyfish to long-horned unicornfish, the wall is also a nursery for baby fishes, flapping their fins madly just to stay in one place. The current sweeps us on and we enter the coral garden at Yolanda Reef. Huge Gorgonian fans wave as though in the wind, while bunches of broccoli sprout up alongside giant mushroom shapes. My buddy prods me and I turn to see a turtle chomping steadily on the coral; a little closer and I can hear the crunch over my own Darth Vader breathing. We drift along, joined now by a metre-long Napoleon wrasse, with its comical, humped head and sad swivelling eye that follows us closely.

need to know

Diving at Ras Mohammed is arranged year-round by dozens of dive schools. One of the best is Red Sea Diving College in Na'ama Bay (Ⓦ www. redseacollege.com).

Around the corner is the wreck of the Yolanda itself, now assimilated by the sea and encrusted with coral layers camouflaging crocodile- and scorpionfish, its cargo of toilets adorned with stinging green fire corals. A blue-spotted ray rises from the sandy bottom and flaps gracefully away. Looking at my gauge, I realize my air's nearly finished; time to re-enter the world above.

On the right track:

watching hornbills

in The Gambia

9

Just like its people, the avian population of this small West African nation are a welcoming lot. There's a remarkable abundance and variety of birds to be found, and a great many are colourful, conspicuous individuals with a "look at me!" attitude – it's bird nerd heaven. Spotting them is as easy as stepping out onto your veranda, as every hotel garden is alive with jaunty little finches, doves, sunbirds and glossy starlings, all far more colourful and alluring than their European counterparts. But the adventurous will want to hire a guide and head off on the kind of walk where you get burrs in your socks and need frequent swigs from your water bottle. In some areas, you can clock up a hundred or more species in a few hours: common wetland birds such as kingfishers, pelicans, herons and egrets, and savannah-dwellers like vultures and rollers are practically guaranteed – as are my favourites, the hornbills.

As endearing as they are faintly ridiculous, hornbills' beaks seem too large for their bodies, and their flapping, gliding flight looks nothing short of haphazard. What's more, they take parental paranoia to grand extremes: if it's breeding season (July and August), you may see a male incarcerating his female and her brood in a nest sealed with mud, high up in a tree, where they'll stay until the young are strong enough to survive on their own.

The most lugubrious fellow of all is the Abyssinian ground hornbill. Nearly a metre tall, cloaked in black and with a beak of gothic proportions, it strides through the open grassland with the undignified haste of an undertaker who's late for an urgent appointment. It's by far the largest – and the most impressive – of the hornbills, so if you manage to spot one, you've really scored. And before you know it, you'll be posting gloating field notes on the internet like a true convert.

need to know

The prime birdwatching areas include the Tanbi Wetlands, Abuko Nature Reserve, Brufut Woods, Marakissa and Janjanbureh. Birding guides can be hired locally; operators such as Birdfinders (ⓦ www.birdfinders.co.uk) offer specialist tours.

10 Tracking tigers in Bandhavgarh, India

need to know To see tigers in Bandhavgarh, contact Discovery Initiatives (🌐 www.discoveryinitiatives.com). For ground arrangements in India, including accommodation, try Royal Expeditions (🌐 www.royalexpeditions.com).

26

After several failed attempts, my quest to see the perfect wild tiger — any wild tiger, in fact — took me to Bandhavgarh national park in the heart of Madya Pradesh. I wasn't optimistic. India's tiger population is suffering from a poaching epidemic and numbers are thought to have fallen as low as 500, down from 50,000 at the beginning of the 1950s. But Bandhavgarh (which has the highest relative tiger density of all India's reserves) exceeded all my wildest dreams.

On our first drive, we saw two cubs lying quietly in a dried-up riverbed, enjoying the evening sun. Next morning, having trans-shipped to the back of an elephant, I saw their mother from three metres up, looking down at a huge, baleful face, framed in the long grass like a Rousseau painting. It was a strange, almost eerie experience, and when we had to move on, I felt a huge sense of loss.

The following evening, as we headed back from the park, a large male crossed the road in front of our jeep, so close that we almost collided with him. He paused for a second to look at us from the side of the road, then made off into the bush - we heard him roaring as he went deeper into the forest, checking his territory for intruders.

The last sighting was on my final day. We had parked by the side of a small lake, its perimeter surrounded by undergrowth, and with a steep, clear slope leading to the water's edge. As we waited, a single fully grown female came out of the trees, sauntered down the slope, went down on her haunches and stretched out her neck to drink. After five minutes, she pushed back and sloped off into the brush. That evening later, still dazed by the experience, I was on the overnight train back to Delhi. As we rumbled through the night, I reflected that at a time when India's tigers are threatened as never before, this majestic animal is alive and flourishing — in Bandhavgarh at least.

11 Frolicking
with fur seals in Chile

Reaching the Juan Fernández archipelago – three volcanic crags way out in the Pacific – is an adventure in itself: three hours from Santiago de Chile in a juddering twin-propeller plane, a half-hour trudge down a dusty track, and a two-hour ride in a leaky fishing-boat just get to the midget capital of Juan Bautista. The first inhabitants you see are a small welcoming party of endemic Juan Fernández fur seals, which wait faithfully for each planeload of visitors in the rocky cove below the airstrip. Wildlife certainly knows how to forgive – until the early twentieth century, islanders slaughtered the seals for their prized pelts, butchering hundreds of thousands and bringing the species to the brink of extinction, but since hunting became illegal, careful conservation has brought the numbers of these photogenic little mammals to over 10,000.

$\mathcal{R}eassured$ that accustoming the seals to human contact doesn't threaten their survival, we donned wetsuits, clambered into another fishing smack and headed for one of the biggest colonies. As we floundered around in our fins and snorkels, our hosts – especially the endearing pups, with their wide-eyed innocent looks – showed us just why the water is their kingdom. It was a truly hands-on exercise – body contact is definitely encouraged and the seals somehow manage to be slippery and cuddly at the same time. While they performed endless somersaults, pikes, tucks and twists around, below and over us, we simultaneously tried to float, signal to the fishermen to take our photo and stay away from the huge grandfather bull. His blustering snorts suggested that his grandchildren were getting too familiar with us, but guide Marcelo said it was just his way of saying hello. And as we chugged away into the sunset it also seemed to be his way of saying goodbye – but not, we hoped, good riddance.

need to know

For information about how to get to the archipelago (some 800km due west of Valparaíso), visit ⓦwww.islarobinsoncrusoe.cl (in Spanish only). The Refugio Náutico on Robinson Crusoe Island, run by Marcelo Rossi and Mónica Quevedo (ⓔrefugionautico@123.cl), offers accommodation and seal trips.

12
UP CLOSE WITH ALLIGATORS

on the Anhinga trail, Florida

Stepping onto the concreted Anhinga trail, you can't help but doubt its reputation as serious gator territory. Leading straight from a car park and with a friendly little visitor centre at its head, the half-mile circular pathway smacks of the type of "nature trail" on which you'd be lucky to catch sight of a sparrow. But don't judge it hastily, as the Everglades is full of surprises.

Located way down in Florida's tropical south, the Everglades National Park covers 1.5 million acres of sawgrass-covered marshland and swamp, the largest subtropical wilderness in the United States and the perfect home for the American alligator. So as you stroll along admiring the exotic birdlife, don't let your guard down: all around you, massive carnivorous reptiles are lurking in the shallows, blending effortlessly into their surroundings. Almost comically prehistoric-looking, they sunbathe inches from the path or sometimes even stretched across it, motionless and slit-eyed, with seemingly hundreds of long, pointed teeth glinting in the hot Floridian sun.

The sheer number of lazing alligators is remarkable, but your effortless proximity to them is even more incredible. In fact, you nearly forget you're in the wild – it all seems far too zoo-like (or even museum-esque, since the animals don't stir); and then, almost before you realize it, and with truly incredible speed, an alligator moves – and the enjoyable awe and excitement you were feeling morphs into sheer terror. When they take to the water and adopt that classic alligator pose – only eyes, teeth and powerful, ridged tail visible as they glide quietly and quickly towards their prey – it's nigh-on impossible to stop yourself from leaping away down the path, burning to tell someone of your near-death experience.

need to know

The Everglades (ⓦ www.nps.gov/ever) are easy driving distance from both Miami (60km) and Naples (30km); it's best to visit during the dry season (Nov–April), when wildlife is concentrated in the few remaining wet areas. For information on guided walks and other activities, check the visitor centres at the entrances and within the park.

3

On the hoof:
Tracking rhino in Namibia

Did you know that the footprint of a black rhino can measure a full 30cm from toe to hefty heel?

Nor did I until I was standing in the middle of one in northern Namibia's Damaraland, my size nines dwarfed by the dusty imprint. A big male had passed here in the night, maybe as little as two hours ago. Our guide finished inspecting the considerable pile of dung teetering on the trail a few metres up ahead, slung his high-calibre rifle onto his shoulder and gestured for us to move on. We were heading east, in the direction of the tracks, for a rendezvous with a BMW-sized beast.

Damaraland is the only place in the world where you can find free-roaming black rhino. But you've got to know where to look. And the trackers from Palmwag – a mobile tented camp set amidst the grassy plains and light scrub of a million-acre private reserve – know exactly where to look. Noticing a stack of steaming spores is easy enough; spotting an acacia bush that's been crumpled by the hooked lips of a browsing black rhino isn't – and it's that sort of proficiency that pretty much guarantees you sneaking up on one just a few hours after leaving camp.

Rhinos have terrible eyesight, but their hearing and sense of smell are acute. As we approach a mother and her calf from downwind, the previously innocuous dry scrub suddenly becomes one giant, crackling boobytrap. We inch ourselves closer and closer, until we can make out oxpecker birds picking insects off the mother's back. She's immense, yet beautiful – 900 kilos of rippling muscle, ribs shifting as she digests the shrubbery. No one talks. I don't breathe. And then they have moved on, and we start talking – and breathing – again.

need to know

Palmwag Rhino Camp is run by Wilderness Safaris (ⓦ www.wilderness -safaris.com) in conjunction with Save the Rhino (ⓦ www.rhino-trust .org.na), a non-profit conservation trust. A double en-suite tent costs $600 per night, which includes all meals, jeep safaris and rhino tracking. A portion of every guest's revenue goes to Save the Rhino.

14 Kiwi-spotting
in Trounson Kauri Park, New Zealand

They're elusive creatures, these kiwi. In fact, New Zealand's national bird is so rare that it's almost never seen other than at the half-dozen places where guided night safaris raise the odds considerably. Heading out on foot, you hear the piercing cry of the male cutting through the inky darkness, closely followed by the husky female reply, but neither has yet seen fit to show its pointy face. The eeriness of their plaintive calls is enhanced by the ghostly presence of kauri trunks, vast walls of bark climbing to the dense canopy high above, with an understorey of slender tree ferns further blocking out the stars.

I can sense the kiwi are nearby, but these things can't be rushed. Not so long ago you'd have been lucky to hear them at all, as introduced stoats, rats, possums and feral cats and dogs had decimated numbers. But Trounson is one of several "mainland islands" where this diminutive relative of the ostrich is being brought back from the brink of extinction, with intensive trapping and poisoning keeping predator numbers low enough to allow indigenous species to flourish. And it's not just kiwi that benefit. Our guide introduces us to the ruru – a native owl known as the "morepork" for the sound of its haunting call – as well as the palm-sized, carnivorous kauri snail and the scary-looking, grasshopper-like weta, which can grow up to 10cm long. They're not dangerous, but no one wants to get too close.

Finally, a gentle scuffling in the leaf litter comes closer and we get our first glimpse of a North Island brown kiwi, its slender beak probing the ground for food. Seemingly unconcerned by our presence, it wanders closer, its shaggy pelt looking more like fur than feathers. Then someone makes an unexpected move and the kiwi takes fright, skittering off into the darkness. Initial disappointment soon fades as another makes itself visible. That's it for the night, but even two sightings seems a rare privilege.

need to know

The Trouson Kauri Park is in Northland, around 200km north of Auckland. The two-hour guided night walk is run from the **Kauri Coast Top 10 Holiday Park** (☏09/439 0621, ⓦwww.kauricoasttop10. co.nz). It takes place every evening (weather permitting) and costs NZ$20.

An indistinct crackle on the ranger's radio broke the peace of our unhurried journey back to the lodge.

Danie translated over his shoulder, ear straining for more reports as he cajoled the Land Rover into picking up a bit more speed. "Two of the unattached young lions are on the move. This is their territory and we've had an idea for a few days that there was another male trying to move in. There's a bit of light from the moon tonight. There could be a rumble." The radio crackled again and we took a sharp turning. "Hold on," said Danie. "They're heading for the waterhole."

We drove hard for a few minutes. The sunset had all but drained from our surroundings, twilight dimming to evening monochrome. At the waterhole there was another vehicle. We drew alongside softly. A ranger in the same uniform as Danie shook his head quickly, then motioned with his hands that we take different routes.

Every movement in the bush made us twitch. The Land Rover bumped slowly over the rutted track.

We came round a corner and stopped suddenly. Danie flicked off his headlights, and with his foot on the clutch slid the gearstick into reverse. The lions were thirty metres away.

They sat on their haunches, peering into the bush away from us, their dark manes bristling. By comparison, the pride we'd seen earlier that day seemed lethargic and uninterested.

No one dared breathe. One of the lions lifted his head and, starting from somewhere around the end of his tail, let out a grumbling, tumbling growl which built into a massive, full-throated primal roar. The sound left the air around us shaking.

A reply rose from further away. Our pair pushed up onto all fours, then moved off purposefully. In seconds they had slipped into the dark shadows of the bush.

"Good luck, guys," said Danie. He flicked on the lights. "I think we'd best leave them to it."

15

LOOKING FOR LIONS IN MADIKWE, SOUTH AFRICA

A lion let out a grumbling, tumbling growl which built into a massive, full-throated primal roar.

need to know

Only a handful of game reserves in South Africa are large enough to accommodate free-ranging lions. Madikwe (ⓦwww .tourismnorthwest.co.za/madikwe) is one, though you can only visit if staying at one of its private lodges; the excellent Jaci's (ⓦwww.madikwe.com).

16 Polar-bear safaris, Canada

❋ **need to know**
You can fly to Churchill from Winnipeg with Calm Air (☎ 204/778-6471; ⊛ www.calmair.com). Tundra buggy trips cost around CDN$80 per day, or you can book an all-inclusive five-day bear-spotting package with Wildlife Adventures (☎ 204/949-2050, ⊛ www.wildlifeadventures .com) for around CDN$3000.

❄ For six weeks from the beginning of October, as temperatures drop below zero and winds gust to 65km per hour, hundreds of polar bears converge around Churchill, Manitoba, a remote town in Canada's far north that quite justifiably claims to be the "polar bear capital of the world". Yet the bears are really only passing through, killing time while waiting for the ice to refreeze on the adjacent vastness of Hudson Bay where they spend most of their lives, lying in wait at blowholes to secure themselves a seal dinner with a quick swipe of a clawed paw.

❄ These few months spent inland before the bay refreezes is the high point of the bears' social calendar, and the annual gathering of these normally solitary animals also attracts groups of hardy visitors to Churchill. Swaddled in multiple layers of clothing, would-be bear-spotters strike out in high-riding, giant-tyred tundra buggies which take them to within a thirty metres of the world's largest land carnivores. Sometimes, given their natural curiosity, bears will saunter over for a quick investigatory sniff, providing plenty of close-range photo opportunities. But many males are likely to be preoccupied by sparring with one another so as to establish a pecking order for food and mates: they touch noses, briefly lock jaws and growl before standing on their hind legs to throw gentlemanly chest-punches.

❄ Eventually, one will concede, rolling onto his back, legs straight in the air, while the victor shows remarkable restraint and backs off swiftly. Females with cubs steer well clear of these shenanigans, as their offspring tend to imitate their every move. This produces an element of choreographed comedy: when the mother digs for kelp, so will the cubs; if she chases away a male (lest he eats her baby), the little whippersnappers will charge too. And in so doing they provide an unbeatable show for the spectators – though the holy grail is the unusual and touching moment of spotting a mother lying prone in a snowbank to nurse her cubs.

17 *Jungle Operatics:* lemurs in Madagascar

Close your eyes and imagine the haunting song of a humpback whale; add heat, humidity and air infused with damp vegetation and moss that tingles your nasal passages. Sounds improbable, doesn't it? Now open your eyes: you're in a Madagascan rainforest listening to a group of indri, the largest of the island's lemurs, proclaiming rights to their territories like arboreal opera singers.

This is the sound of Madagascar. In the early mornings, the forests of Andasibe-Mantadia National Park ring out with the indri's eerie, wailing chorus. It wafts through the canopy in wave after glorious wave, sending shivers down your spine and making every nerve-end jangle.

A number of Indri family groups here have become thoroughly accustomed to people. With the help of a local guide, they're easily seen, and their cute teddy bear looks, striking black-and-white coats and comically inquisitive manner make them hugely endearing – most people fall for them immediately. When you first come upon them, the indri are likely to be high in the canopy, shrouded by a veil of foliage, but it pays to be patient and wait (something many people don't do), as they regularly descend to lower levels and are quite happy to sit and munch their leafy breakfasts while you watch in wonder from close by.

Eleven other lemur species live in the national park, and there's a good chance of seeing several of these, too. One of the most remarkable is the diademed sifaka, its orange and silver fur contrasting vividly with the dark recesses of the forest. I've seen both indri and diademed sifakas many, many times, but it's impossible to tire of what I think are the most beautiful primates on the planet: on each occasion, the intense thrill of tracking them down has always lived up to the excitement of my initial sighting.

need to know

September to December is the best time to visit, when the lemurs have had their young and when most other wildlife is active. The best way to see Madagascar is an organized wildlife tour.

Try Papyrus Tours (☎01405 785 232, ⓦwww.papyrustours.co.uk), the Ultimate Travel Company (☎020 7386 4646, ⓦwww.ultimatetravelcompany.co.uk) or Wildlife Worldwide (☎0845 130 6982).

The Kings
of Komodo,
Indonesia

18

need to know

Most trips to Komodo (ⓦ komodonationalpark.org) are organized from Labuanbajo, on the coast of neighbouring Flores. Two-day trips begin at $40 per boat per day including food. Permits are around $3.

There are few expeditions more disquieting than visiting Indonesia's Komodo Island. Approaching by boat, it appears staggeringly beautiful – the archetypal tropical hideaway. But doubts about the sagacity of what you're about to do surface as soon as you step ashore and discover that you're sharing the beach with the local deer population: if they're too frightened to spend much time in the interior, is it entirely wise for you to do so?

Your unease only grows at the nearby national park office, as you're briefed about the island's most notorious inhabitant. From the tip of a tail so mighty that one swish could knock a buffalo off its feet, to a mouth that drips with saliva so foul that most bite victims die from infected wounds rather than the injuries themselves, Komodo dragons are 150kg of pure reptilian malevolence.

They are also – on Komodo at least – quite numerous, and it doesn't take long before you come across your first dragon, usually basking motionless on a rock or up a tree (among an adult dragon's more unpleasant habits is a tendency to feed on the young, so adolescents often seek sanctuary in the branches).

... a mouth that drips with saliva so foul that most bite victims die from infected wounds rather than the injuries themselves ...

So immobile are they during the heat of the day that the only proof that they're still alive is an occasional flick of the tongue, usually accompanied by a globule of viscous drool that drips and hangs from the side of their mouths. Indeed, it's this docility that encourages you – possibly against your better judgement – to edge closer, until eventually those of sufficient nerve are almost within touching distance.

And it's only then, as you crouch delicately on your haunches and examine the loose folds of battle-scarred skin, the dark, eviscerating talons and the cold, dead eyes of this natural-born killer, that you can fully appreciate how fascinating these creatures really are, and that there is nothing, but nothing, so utterly, compellingly revolting on this planet.

PLATYPUS
-looking for a duck-billed mammal in Australia

There are plenty of animals which you just couldn't make up – think of squid, for instance, with their ten arms, jet-propelling body, human-like eyes, parrot's beak and communication system that consists of rapid changes of colour. So it's a little surprising that when the first dried, stuffed specimens of Australia's platypus were examined by British scientists in the early nineteenth century, they insisted it was a badly thought-out hoax made from bits of other animals sewn together. In fact, it was even weirder than they realized: not only do platypus genuinely look like a cross between a duck and an otter, but they lay eggs, requiring a whole new scientific order of mammals – monotremes – to be created.

All the more reason, then, to head up to the hills of eastern Australia and make a point of tracking one down. Platypus live in rivers and are reasonably common, but as they're extremely timid, vanishing at the slightest movement, you'll need a lot of patience to see one – dusk and dawn are the best times to look. And as they're under 30cm in length, your first reaction on seeing one will be "they're not as big as I thought". One of the best ways to track them is to follow the trail of mud rising off the bottom of a stream, caused as their rubbery bills rummage along the bottom in search of shrimps and beetles. Once they've found a beakful they bob to the surface to eat, lying flat on their fronts with their webbed feet splayed as they chew and glance nervously around – then it's a swift roll headfirst down to the bottom again. In winter, you might see a courting pair chasing each other around the water in tight circles; after mating, the female walls herself into a burrow, dug into the bank above the waterline, to wait for the young to hatch. And if you're lucky, you might see the young following her in a line, each holding on to the tail of the one in front.

need to know

One of the best places to see platypus in the wild is at Broken River in Eungella National Park, Queensland, where there's a viewing platform built over the river and the platypus, fairly used to being watched by humans, are not too timid. The park lies 80km inland from the coastal city of Mackay and is easily reached by road.

GORILLAS

in **Kahuzi-Biega** **20**
National Park,
Democratic Republic of the

CONGO

"If a gorilla charges,
stand still"

We set out on foot from the park headquarters at Tsivanga, and spent the next two hours following a wildly gushing watercourse upstream, climbing steeply all the time. The trackers were somewhere up ahead of us, and messages were passed regularly on the radio. After a particularly strenuous uphill stretch, clutching at roots and branches to drag ourselves up a near-vertical slope, we heard a sudden stentorian roar as a fully grown male gorilla (known to the guides as Chimanuka) burst out of the undergrowth. I knew what I was meant to do. The park's chief guide had briefed us: "If a gorilla charges, stand still," he said. "Lower your head. Look submissive." He stared pointedly at me. "Better wear a hat. If they see your fair hair, they may think you're another silverback."

Yes, I knew what to do all right. But when Chimanuka sprang from the bush in all his glory, his solid muscle rippling in the dappled sunlight, I didn't stand my ground and lower my head. I jumped behind our pygmy tracker and held my breath. This was a huge and magnificent animal, weighing 200 kilograms and, when standing upright, some 1.7 metres tall – I had never seen anything like it before.

Chimanuka must have charged us half a dozen times that morning. He seemed to enjoy it. The pattern went as follows: a charge would be followed by a period of chewing the cud. He would sit on his haunches, rolling his eyes and swiping the available vegetation with his long prehensile arms so as to grab any accessible fruits or succulent stalks. After ten minutes or so, he would rise and turn away from us to show off his magnificent coat (it really is silver), before crashing off again through the undergrowth. Shock and awe. That's what you feel when you first see a gorilla in the wild.

need to know

For information on how you can assist with conservation efforts to protect the gorillas in the Eastern Congo, including possible visits to Kahuzi-Biega National Park, contact the Gorilla Organisation (ⓦ www.gorillas.org). You can also arrange trips in Rwanda; visit ⓦ www.discoveryinitiatives.com.

SIZE MATTERS:

In search of the world's longest snake,

21

Venezuela

Need to know

*Los Llanos is reached from San Fernando de Apure, about an hours'
flight from Caracas. The best places to stay are Hato El Cedral (𝕎www
.hatocedral.com) and Hato El Frío (𝕎www.elfrioeb.com), isolated ranches
two to three hours' drive of San Fernando de Apure; rates include food,
lodging and guided excursions into the floodplains. The easiest time to
find anacondas is in the dry season (Nov–May).*

At an average of seven metres long and weighing up to 250kg, you'd think it'd be impossible for the green anaconda to find somewhere to hide. But gazing out over Venezuala's Los Llanos floodplain, probably the best place in the world to find these super-sized serpents, all I can see are a couple of scarlet ibis and a herd of capybara. But Felipe, my guide, assures me that they are out there, and we set off into the wetlands.

Anacondas entwine their prey in a horrific hug, unhinging their jaws and swallowing it whole; digesting their meal headfirst is easier for them, Felipe tells me, as their prey's limbs tend to fold this way. With this nugget of gratuitously detailed information fresh in my mind, I follow him closely, keeping a comforting rodent shield of capybaras – the anaconda's snack of choice – between myself and the water. Fed by the Orinoco river, Los Llanos spills across 300,000 square kilometres of flooded savannah – almost a third of the country – but Felipo seems to know exactly which patch of indiscriminate reeds to head for. His expertise is complemented by the very latest in anaconda detection tools – a stick – and he sets to work, prodding the swampy foliage in front of him at regular (and cautious) intervals.

It seems to work – after half an hour, Felipe strikes ophidian oil. Quick as a flash, he grabs the tail; Carlos, his assistant, grabs the head, and the battle begins. The beast is big: a good 3.5-metre-long, I estimate (from a good four metres away). I pluck up enough courage to inch closer until I can reach out and touch it. It's like patting a wet tyre: cold, damp and dense. After a few more minutes of sizing it up, the two men let it go, and it ripples off into the water. And then it's just Felipe, Carlos and me, and the seemingly endless watery horizon of Los Llanos.

49

22
Going ape
in
Borneo

They're orange, they hang in trees, but they're not a fruit. Hairy rubber balls of creatures with a judo grip and a sense of humour, orangutans are our nearest evolutionary cousins and the original "men of the forest". Like all the great apes, they're getting extremely rare, and are found only on the huge island of Borneo, but there are still places where it's possible to see them fairly easily, in something approaching their natural state.

A research centre dedicated to reintroducing baby orangutans orphaned by the pet trade into the wild, Camp Leakey is about five hours by klotok boat up the Sekonyer river from the tiny port of Kumai. It's a wonderful journey, past banks fringed with the huge fronds of nipa palms, then along increasingly narrow, tea-coloured tributaries flanked by ever-thicker jungle. Sitting on the klotok's flat roof as it chugs slowly along, there's a lot to look out for – the log-like head of a gharial crocodile, sinking without a ripple as the boat nears; proboscis monkeys making wild leaps between branches and occasionally jumping straight into the water for a

swim, their oversized noses bobbing along; and the quiet shadows of gibbons moving swiftly through the treetops. And there, it's your first view of an orangutan, a great blob of orange fur hanging on to a rattan vine above the water, trying to grab a pandanus fruit. Docking at a boardwalk a few minutes later, you're met by another one, much younger, who grabs you with an irresistibly strong but gentle hand, and climbs onto your back to hug you like a rucksack. There's no shifting him, so you carry him up to the boardwalk to a clearing where the orphans get a feed of bananas every evening.

He hitches a ride until a ranger appears, and then jumps down and scoots off towards the dozen others waiting impatiently for their supper to arrive. And once it does, and he's eaten his fill, it's straight up into the treetops for a snooze without a backward glance.

need to know

Kumai is about an hour from Pangkalanbun, where you must first pick up permits for your visit from the police and PKA (National Parks) office, then arrange a klotok. More information, including costs and details of accommodation in the park, can be found at ⓦ www .orangutan.org.

23 SWIMMING WITH TURTLES

in the

A cluster of granite islands enveloped in deep-green tropical

SEYCHELLES

vegetation and edged with beaches of blindingly white sand that's so fine it squeaks when you walk across it, the Seychelles are the nearest thing on earth to the Garden of Eden. The turquoise waters of the surrounding Indian Ocean are also one of the best places in the world to see marine turtles, especially the hawksbill, once severely endangered by the trade in its beautifully patterned shells, which were used to make combs, spectacle frames and the like. With most of the Seychelles' waters now a marine reserve, hawksbill numbers have bounced back locally, though the species is still threatened worldwide.

The best place to see them is on their home turf, so don mask, snorkel and fins – or full scuba gear – and get into the sea. Watching them flapping effortlessly past you into the blue is an incredible spectacle; they're sometimes curious, sometimes indifferent, but usually wary of letting you get too close – best to catch them asleep under coral overhangs or in shallow caves, where they can spend up to an hour dozing. If you're not prepared to get wet, the best time to see them is the October–February nesting season when, just after dark, you'll find females heaving themselves up the beaches to just above the high-tide line before using their hind flippers to scoop out a deep pit. They then lay about fifty round, parchment-shelled eggs before shovelling all the sand back on top of them and making their way back down to the water. The eggs incubate in the sand (the sex of the entire clutch is determined by the surrounding temperature) until the young hatch around ten weeks later. Perfect hawksbills in miniature, they dig themselves out of the nest after dark and, using the moon as a guide, scuttle frenetically down the beach toward the sea like an army of wind-up bath toys.

need to know

The Seychelles (ⓦ www
.seychelles.com) is a group
of mostly small islands; the
capital, Victoria, is on the
largest, Mahé. Many resorts
offer turtle-watching trips in
season; one of the easiest
places to see them is Co
Island.

24 Meeting the Monarchs in Mexico

need to know

The best place to see the butterflies is in the official butterfly sanctuary above the village of El Rosario (mid-Nov to mid-March daily 9am–5pm; $2; ☎ 01-800/450-2300, ⊛ www.turismomichoacan .gob.mx). There are buses from Mexico City (5–6 daily; 3hr) or Morelia (20 daily; 2hr 30min) to Zitácuaro, from where buses run to the sanctuary in the migration season.

Early morning in the mountains of Michoacán. There's a stillness in the wooded glades and a delicate scent of piney resin in the air. Mostly oyamel firs, the trees are oddly coated in a scrunched orange blanket – some kind of fungus? Diseased bark? Then the sun breaks through the mist and thousands of butterflies swoop from the branches to bathe in the sunlight, their patterned orange-and-black wings looking like stained-glass windows or Turkish rugs – the original Mexican wave. The forest floor is carpeted with them. Branches buckle and snap under their weight. And there's a faint noise, a pitter-patter like gentle rain – the rarely heard sound of massed butterflies flapping their wings.

The annual migration of hundreds of millions of monarch butterflies from North America to this small area of central Mexico – no more than 96 kilometres square – is one of the last mysteries of the scientific world. For years, their winter home was known only to the locals, but in 1975, two determined American biologists finally pinpointed the location, and now visitors (mainly Mexican) flock in during the season to witness one of nature's most impressive spectacles. In the silence of the forest sanctuary, people stand stock-still for hours at a time, almost afraid to breathe as millions of butterflies fill the air, brushing delicately against faces and alighting briefly on hands.

No one is entirely clear why the butterflies have chosen this area. Some say it's the oyamel's needle-like leaves, ideal for the monarch's hooked legs to cling onto; or that the cool highland climate slows down their metabolism and allows them to rest and lay down fat before their arduous mating season. The Aztecs, however, had other ideas, believing that the butterflies – which arrive in Mexico shortly after the Day of the Dead on November 1 – were the returning souls of their fallen warriors, clad in the bright colours of battle.

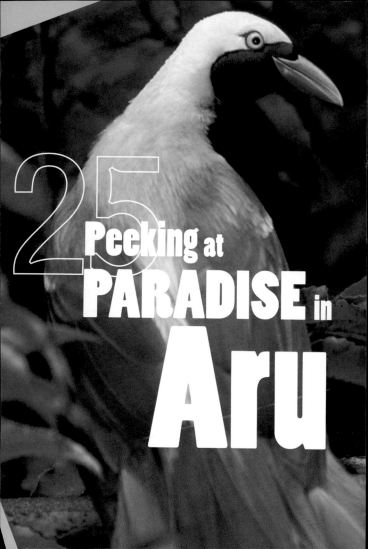

25

Peeking at PARADISE in Aru

So here I was in the middle of the jungle in Aru, at the end of the end of everywhere in the southeastern Indonesian province of Maluku, trying to find cenderawasih, the greater bird of paradise. These are gorgeous creatures, about the size of a thrush and with a similarly brown body, but one topped by a metallic green cap and, in males, a fantastic fountain of long, fluffy-looking golden feathers, which are proudly swished and shaken in territorial dancing displays.

But they were proving elusive: this was my fourth attempt within a year, after the others had ended in ferry strandings, political violence and a plane crash. I had now spent three days being taken ever-deeper into the forest's vine-tangled depths by hunters who I could barely communicate with, leaving me with tick bites aplenty but no sign of birds of paradise. We hadn't even heard their noisy "wok-wok-wok-wok" call, which sounds as melodic as a tin alarm clock going off, and has caused locals to brand them burung bodoh, the stupid bird, because the racket makes them easy to track down and shoot.

But I was having fun, and now it was 6am on day five, my last, and I was being led into the forest once again by the sixty-year-old Bapak Gusti. He'd collared me in the village the evening before and casually mentioned that he owned a tree, just a short walk away, where the birds displayed every morning. I had nothing to lose by this point; my only worry was that this – like all the other "short walks" I had undertaken here – would actually last six hours, and the boat out would leave without me. But I was wrong: within twenty minutes, he had led me to a tree where, on a bare branch 30m up in the canopy, three male birds of paradise were displaying their hearts out, their plumage glowing as bright as the sunlight which brushed the treetops.

need to know

Aru's major settlement, Dobo, is two days from the Maluku district capital, Ambon, with Pelni, the Indonesian state shipping line. As there are no roads on Aru, transport to outlying villages is by boat only, and you'll need to arrange a private charter in Dobo.

WOK WOK WOK WOK

Ultimate
experiences
Wildlife
Adventures
miscellany

1 Bigger, older, stronger

Growing up to nearly four metres long and weighing in at 160 tonnes, the blue whale is the **largest animal in the world**. Its diet is made up almost entirely of tiny, shrimp-like krill, one of the smallest animals in the world; blue whales will consume around four to six tonnes of krill in a single day. Giant Galápagos tortoises are the **longest living animal on the planet**; Harriet, a tortoise who was picked up on the Galápagos Islands by Charles Darwin, was 176 when she died at Australia's Queensland Reptile Park in June 2006. The **strongest animal on earth** is the rhinoceros beetle, which can carry up to 850 times its body weight on its back.

2 Different class

According to most modern classification systems, animals count as one of five groups, or kingdoms. The **animal kingdom** is divided into two sub-groups: **invertebrates** – any animal without a spinal column (97 percent of all animal species) – and **vertebrates**, those that do have a spinal column. These are both then divided into **phyla**, which are then further divided into **classes**, classes into **orders**, orders into **families**, families into **genera** and, finally, each genus is divided into **species**.

▶▶ An example classification: the hippopotamus

Kingdom: Animalia
Phylum: Chordata
Class: Mammalia
Order: Artiodactyla
Family: Hippopotamidae
Genus: Hippopotamus
Species: H. amphibius

The nomenclature used to designate animals is known as the **Linnaean system** after the Swedish botanist who devised it; its two name categories – genus and species – are largely derived from Latin and Greek descriptions of the animal's characteristics. For example, the jackass penguin's scientific name is speniscus demersus – speniscus comes from the Greek for "little wedge", a reference to penguins' wings, while demersus is from the Latin demergo, meaning "I sink," a possible allusion to the depths to which the birds can dive.

3 Bird bonanza

The **Pipeline Road**, a 24-kilometre-long trail in the heart of Parque Nacional Soberanía, Panama, holds the world record for the highest number of bird species identified in a 24-hour period: in 1996, the Audubon Society counted an incredible **360** different specimens.

4 Following the herd

▶▶ Five great migrations

Wildebeest A continual 800km clockwise movement across the Serengeti plains in Tanzania and into Kenya.

Arctic terns The longest migration on earth: 40,000km from the Arctic to the Antarctic – and back again.

Monarch butterflies An 8000-kilometre return journey from the eastern Rockies to central Mexico.

Grey whales A 16,000-kilometre round-trip from Baja California to the Bering Sea.

Sardines One huge shoal – 15km long, 3500m wide and nearly 40m deep – that annually moves north along the coast of South Africa.

5 Young at heart

Some animals, including most species of **fish**, produce millions of eggs at any one time, releasing them into the ocean and letting them care for themselves in the likelihood that at least a small percentage will make it to adulthood. Others, such as **elephants**, will have just a single offspring, and will invest a huge amount of effort to ensure its survival, caring for their babies for up to six years.

Marsupials, such as kangaroos and koala bears, look after their young in pouches until they're up to four months old. The male seahorse also cares for its offspring in a sack-like pouch which protects them until they're big enough to be released into the sea. The aptly named parent bug is one of only a few insects that guard their young until they are old enough – five or six weeks – to fend for themselves.

▶▶ Pregnancy periods and names for the young

Animal	Gestation period	Name of young
Elephant	3–4 years	Calf
Hawksbill turtle	3–4 months	Hatchling
Duckbilled platypus	2–3 weeks	Puggle
Llama	11–12 months	Cria
Rat	3 weeks	Kitten

6 A distant second

It takes a **cheetah** just over 3 seconds to cover 100m; a **sloth**, on the other hand, needs 12 minutes to haul itself the same distance. **Turtles** are the long-distance runners of the animal world: loggerheads cover some 24,000km during their migration across the Pacific from Japan to Mexico.

"The frog does not drink up the pond in which he lives."

Native American proverb

7 The bear necessities

There are only nine species of bear in the world, including two species of panda. The **American black bear** is the most common, with as many as 750,000 across Canada, the USA and Mexico; the **sun bear** and the **spectacled bear** (the latter being the only bear found in South America) are the rarest.

▶▶ Five bear species and where to spot them

American black bear Yellowstone National Park, USA
Brown bear Carpathian Mountains, Romania
Giant panda Fengtongzhai, China
Sloth bear Daroji, India
Polar bear Svaalbard, Norway

8 The Galápagos Islands

A utopia for wildlife enthusiasts, the Galápagos Islands were discovered in 1535 by the Bishop of Panama, Fray Tomás de Berlanda, but its unique animals only achieved international fame following the visit of **Charles Darwin** in 1835. In 1959, around ninety percent of the Galápagos was designated a national park, and in 1978 the islands were named a World Heritage Site.

It was Darwin's research on the Galápagos – articulated in his major work, **The Origin of Species** – that helped overturn the static view of nature and prove that life-forms evolve. Species on one island, Darwin noted, had marked differences to those on another, meaning that those better able to adapt to their individual environments survived – and evolved. Darwin termed this "**natural selection**" or "**survival of the fittest**".

▶▶ Five famous Galápagos residents

- Giant tortoise
- Frigatebird
- Marine iguana
- Blue-footed booby
- Lava lizard

9 Extreme diets

Camels can last a month without **water**; anacondas can go without **food** for up to a year. Pandas, meanwhile, must spend almost their entire lives eating bamboo, feeding for up to sixteen hours per day in order to get enough nutrients to stay alive.

10 Dangers down under

Aside from the saltwater **crocodiles** that fill the billabongs of Queensland and the Northern Territory, Australia is home to six of the world's ten most **venomous snakes** – including the most dangerous of all, the "fierce snake" or inland taipan, which has enough venom in a single bite to kill a hundred humans. There are also deadly red back and funnel web **spiders**, and even the innocent-looking **duck-billed platypus** has toxic spurs on the back of its legs. You're not much better off in the water, either – if you can avoid the man-eating **sharks** (the great white and the tiger), you've still got a bevy of poisonous **jellyfish** (the box, irukandji and bluebottle) to contend with. And there's also the **blue-ring octopus**, whose lethal bite has no known antidote.

11 The name game

▶▶ Ten names of animal groups

A **bloat** of hippopotamus

A **smack** of jellyfish

A **murder** of ravens

A **surfeit** of skunks

A **bask** of crocodiles

An **array** of hedgehogs

A **flange** of gibbons

A **slew** of sharks

A **business** of ferrets

An **ambush** of tigers

12 Tourism concern

The revenue from tourism can play an important part in driving animal conservation – but not always. The **Maasai Mara** in Kenya, for example, generates more than fifteen percent of the country's tourist revenue, and yet wildebeest numbers fell by more than eighty percent from 1977 to

1997 – and over the next four years (1997–2001), wildlife in the park declined by a further sixty percent.

13 The sky's the limit...

The **common flea** can leap up to 34cm high – more than 113 times its size – and, when trying to find a new host on which it can feed, can do so six hundred times an hour for up to three days at a time.

Fleas are reproductively prolific, with females laying up to 200 eggs in their lifetimes, as well as being voracious eaters, consuming up to 15 times their own body weight in blood each day.

"Lots of people talk to animals. Not many listen, though . . . That's the problem."

Benjamin Hoff, The Tao of Pooh

14 Wildlife playlist

- **Eye of the Tiger**, Survivor
- **Hungry Like the Wolf**, Duran Duran
- **Karma Chameleon**, Culture Club
- **I am the Walrus**, The Beatles
- **The Lion Sleeps Tonight**, The Tokens

15 A whale of a time

There are 77 species of whale, which are split into two groups: **baleen** (those without teeth, whose diet consists of plankton) and **toothed** (whales who hunt and capture prey). Baleen whales, such as blue and humpback whales, have two blowholes; toothed whales, including sperm and killer whales, have one.

▶▶ Five whale species and where to watch them

Sperm whale Kaikoura, New Zealand
Grey whale Baja California, Mexico
Killer whale Península Valdés, Argentina
Pilot whale Gibraltar, Spain
Southern right whale Hermanus, South Africa

16 Dangerous liaisons

The praying mantis is the best known example of an animal that practices **sexual cannibalism** – where the female of the species eats the male before, during or after mating. This decidedly unsafe sex is thought to occur for the benefit of the species as a whole: a female **orb weaver spider** will eat unsuitable males to prevent them from mating with her; the Mantis religiosa species of **praying mantis** requires that the male be decapitated for proper ejaculation to occur; and a female **redback spider** that has eaten her mate will not copulate with another male spider thanks to a sperm plug that the male inserts into the female's abdomen – thus ensuring the reproductive success of the sacrificed male.

"The time will come when men such as I will look on the murder of animals as they now look on the murder of men."

Leonardo da Vinci

17 The sweet smell of success

In January 2006, a couple walking along their local beach in southern Australia found a 15kg ball of **ambergris**, a hardened lump of **sperm whale vomit**. Starting life as a soft, foul-smelling excretion, years of exposure to salt water and sunshine transforms it into a waxy clump with a musky smell – and a prime component in perfume. The couple's discovery was valued at US$300,000.

18 Sacred cows

Thanks to the world's 900 million adherents of Hinduism, the **cow** is perhaps the most revered animal on the planet. Its sacred status can be traced back to Lord Krishna, one of the religion's most important figures, who is said to have appeared as a cowherd.

The **asp**, also known as the Egyptian cobra, was worshipped in ancient Egypt. The snake was seen as a symbol of power, and its image adorned the crown of the pharaohs.

The Native Americans of the Great Plains had such a strong connection with the **buffalo** that they celebrated its spirit in ceremonies and prayers. The religious beliefs of the Sioux revolved around Wakan Tanka, or Great Mystory, an all-pervasive force; tatanka is the Lakota Sioux word for "buffalo".

19 Endangered animals

The **IUCN Red List of Threatened Species** records the conservation status of plant and animal species, an indicator of whether certain species will survive in the future. The status is determined not only by the number remaining, but also by breeding success rates, known threats and the decrease in population over time. In the 2006 Red List, 7725 species were considered threatened; the USA was the worst offender, with 231 extinctions and a further 236 species designated critically endangered, while 18 species had become extinct worldwide since 2000.

▶▶ Five animals on the endangered list

- **Knysna banana frog** South Africa
- **Sumatran rhino** Indonesia
- **Long-legged warbler** Fiji
- **Atlantic northern right whale** Canada and the USA
- **Golden-rumped elephant shrew** Kenya

20 Small is beautiful

The **smallest animal in the world** is a controversial subject. Most scientists believe, however, that the title belongs to Dicopomorpha echmepterygis, a parasitic wasp that measures a minuscule 139 micrometres. One of the smallest mammals is the Kitti's hog-nosed (or bumblebee) bat at around 3cm long,

21 On safari

"**Safari**" is the Kiswahili word for "journey"; it entered the English language in the nineteenth century, when white Europeans visited Africa on big-game hunting expeditions.

Lion, black rhino, elephant, leopard and buffalo are known in safari circles as the **Big Five**, a phrase originally coined by hunters in recognition of them being the most dangerous – and, consequently, the most sought-after – game, but which is now used as a means of attracting animal-spotting tourists.

▶▶ Five great African safari destinations

Serengeti Legendary Tanzanian park, whose open savannah and acacia woodlands are filled with huge herds of wildebeest, zebra and gazelle – and their accompanying predators (lions, leopards and African hunting dogs).

Okavango Delta This latticework of reed-filled lagoons, lakes and flooded channels in northwest Botswana is the largest inland delta in the world, and is best explored on the back of an African elephant.

Kruger National Park The size of Wales, South Africa's Kruger packs nearly 150 species of mammals – from reedbucks to rhinos – and more than 500 kinds of bird into its varied terrain.

Etosha National Park This immense salt pan in northern Namibia provides spectacular game viewing in the dry season, from antelopes to giraffes, rhinos and lions.

Maasai Mara The best animal reserve in Kenya, with hundreds of different species – including the Big Five – roaming its rolling grasslands.

22 You're not from around here . . .

Man has been introducing animal and plant species to all corners of the globe for hundreds of years, usually with the same catastrophic effects. **Invasive species** can prove affect disastrous to the native wildlife, preying on them, competing with them for food, introducing illnesses or destroying their habitat.

▶▶ Five invasive species

Beavers Introduced to Argentine Tierra del Fuego from Canada in an attempt to start a fur-farming industry, beaver dams have flooded mountain valleys and flatlands.

Grey squirrels Brought to the UK from the United States, greys have virtually wiped out the endemic red squirrel.

Goats Introduced to the Galapagos Islands by British sailors as food, the goats' feeding habits are destroying the natural habitat of the iconic giant tortoise.

Cane toads Introduced to Eastern Australia from South America in order to control the cane beetle, cane toads have no natural predators, and have spread into north Queensland and the Northern Territory. And ironically, their introduction has proved completely pointless, as they can't jump high enough to reach the tops of the cane stalks where their potential prey live.

Possums Brought over to New Zealand from Australia with the aim of establishing a fur industry, they cause enormous damage to native flora and fauna.

23 Monkey business

Dame Jane Goodall, a British primatologist, almost single-handedly changed the way scientists view the ape world. Famous for her studies of **chimpanzees** on the shores of Tanzania's Lake Tanganyika, Goodall was the first person to prove that animals had distinct personalities; she also discovered that chimpanzees fashioned tools and fought long-term wars with rival groups. In 1965, she established the **Gombe Stream Research**

Centre in Tanzania, and in 1977 founded the **Jane Goodall Institute** (ⓦ www.janegoodall.org) to provide support for field research into wild chimpanzees.

American conservationist **Dian Fossey** spent nearly twenty years living among the **mountain gorillas** of the Virunga Volcanoes in central Africa. In 1967, she established the world's first mountain gorilla research centre – the **Karisoke Research Centre** in Rwanda – but it was her autobiographical novel *Gorillas in the Mist*, published in 1983 and subsequently transferred onto the silver screen in 1987, that really brought their plight to a global audience. Fossey spent the latter part of her life waging war on illegal poaching; she was murdered – probably by a poacher – in December 1985 and lies buried in the cemetery next to her beloved gorillas. The **Gorilla Organization** (ⓦ www.gorillas.org) was set up to continue her work.

24 Penguin politics

Emperor penguins huddle together in herds to keep warm in their freezing Antarctic habitat; there can be up to ten adults per square metre at the centre of the huddle, producing enough heat to release a cloud of steam.

The **rockhopper penguin** gets its name from the way it skilfully pogos from boulder to boulder in an effort to reach its cliff-top nest sites.

▸▸ Five penguins and where to view them

Jackass penguin Cape Town, South Africa
Emperor penguin Coulman Island, Antarctica
Fairy penguin Phillip Island, Australia
Magallenic penguin Punta Tombo, Argentina
Yellow-eyed penguin Otago Peninsula, New Zealand

"Wherever man has gone he has created havoc with the balance of nature."

Gerald Durrell

25 The long and the short of it

Spare a thought for poor old Ephemeroptera – the **mayfly**. It spends several years under water as a nymph, but only lives for an hour as an adult; however, with a primary function of reproducing – the male's legs are designed purely to aid mid-air mating – it's quite some sixty minutes . . .

Ultimate
experiences
Wildlife
Adventures
small print

ROUGH GUIDES
give you the complete experience

"Authoritative, practical and refreshingly direct, Rough Guides can't be beat."
Chicago Tribune

Broaden your horizons

www.roughguides.com

ROUGH GUIDES – don't just travel

We hope you've been inspired by the experiences in this book. There are 24 other books in the 25 Ultimate Experiences series, each conceived to whet your appetite for travel and foreverything the world has to offer. As well as covering the globe, the 25s series also includes books on **Journeys, World Food, Adventure Travel, Places to Stay, Ethical Travel,** and **Wonders of the World**.

When you start planning your trip, Rough Guides' new-look guides, maps and phrasebooks are the ultimate companions. For 25 years we've been refining what makes a good guidebook and we now include more colour photos and more information – on average 50% more pages – than any of our competitors. Just look for the sky-blue spines.

Rough Guides don't just travel – we also believe in getting the most out of life without a passport. Since the publication of the bestselling Rough Guides to **The Internet** and **World Music**, we've brought out a wide range of lively and authoritative guides on everything from **Climate Change** to **Hip-Hop**, from **MySpace** to **Film Noir** and from **The Brain** to **The Rolling Stones**.

Publishing information

Rough Guide 25 Ultimate experiences Wildlife Adventures Published May 2007 by Rough Guides Ltd, 80 Strand, London WC2R 0RL

345 Hudson St, 4th Floor,
New York, NY 10014, USA

14 Local Shopping Centre, Panchsheel Park, New Delhi 110017, India

Distributed by the Penguin Group

Penguin Books Ltd,
80 Strand, London WC2R 0RL

Penguin Group (USA)
375 Hudson Street, NY 10014, USA

Penguin Group (Australia)
250 Camberwell Road, Camberwell, Victoria 3124, Australia

Penguin Books Canada Ltd,
10 Alcorn Avenue, Toronto, Ontario, Canada M4V 1E4

Penguin Group (NZ)
67 Apollo Drive, Mairangi Bay, Auckland 1310, New Zealand

Printed in China

© Rough Guides 2007

80pp

A catalogue record for this book is available from the British Library

ISBN: 971-84353-834-9

The publishers and authors have done their best to ensure the accuracy and currency of all the information in **Rough Guide 25 Ultimate experiences Wildlife Adventures**, however, they can accept no responsibility for any loss, injury, or inconvenience sustained by any traveller as a result of information or advice contained in the guide.

1 3 5 7 9 8 6 4 2

Rough Guide credits

Editor: Polly Thomas
Design & picture research: Chloë Roberts, Monica Visca, Andrew Oliver
Cartography: Katie Lloyd-Jones, Maxine Repath

Cover design: Diana Jarvis, Chloë Roberts
Production: Aimee Hampson, Katherine Owers
Proofreader: Samantha Cook

The authors

Polly Rodger Brown (Experiences 1, 4, 7, 24) is co-author of the *Rough Guide First-Time Latin America*. **Paul Whitfield** (Experiences 2, 14) is author of the *Rough Guide to Alaska*, and co-author of the *Rough Guide to New Zealand*. **Harry Adès** (Experience 3) is co-author of the *Rough Guide to Ecuador and the Galápagos Islands*. **Keith Drew** (Experiences 5, 13, 21) is a Senior Travel Editor for Rough Guides who has seen all of the Big Five and some very large snakes, too. **Stephen Keeling** (Experience 6) lived in Shanghai for two years. **Kate Berens** (Experience 8) is Rough Guides' Editorial Director and a diving devotee. **Emma Gregg** (Experience 9) is co-author of the *Rough Guide to The Gambia*. **Stanley Johnson** (Experiences 10, 20) is a writer and environmentalist, and a trustee of the Dian Fossey Gorilla Fund. **Andrew Benson** (Experience 11) is co-author of the *Rough Guide to Chile*. **Sarah Eno** (Experience 12) is a Travel Editor for Rough Guides who has holidayed in The Everglades. **Donald Reid** (Experience 15) is co-author of the *Rough Guide to South Africa*. **Christian Williams** (Experience 16) is co-author of the *Rough Guide to Canada*. **Nick Garbutt** (Experience 17) is a wildlife writer and photographer, and also leads tours of the Madagascan rainforests. **Henry Stedman** (Experience 18) is co-author of the *Rough Guide to Indonesia*. **David Leffman** (Experiences 19, 22, 23, 25) is co-author of Rough Guides to Australia and Indonesia.

Picture credits

Fly Less – Stay Longer!

Rough Guides believes in the good that travel does, but we are deeply aware of the impact of fuel emissions on climate change. We recommend taking fewer trips and staying for longer. If you can avoid travelling by air, please use an alternative, especially for journeys of under 1000km/600miles. And always offset your travel at **www.roughguides.com/climatechange**.

Over 70 reference books and hundreds of travel
guides, maps & phrasebooks that cover the world